THE RELENTLESS PRONOUN

Lynne Potts

GLASS LYRE PRESS

Copyright © 2017 Lynne Potts

Paperback ISBN: 978-1-941783-30-6

All rights reserved: except for the purpose of quoting brief passages for review, no part of this book may be reproduced or transmitted in any form or by any means, electronic or mechanical, including photocopying, recording, or by any information storage and retrieval system, without permission in writing from the publisher.

Cover art: © Dunja | Dreamstime.com
Author Photo:
Design & layout: Steven Asmussen
Copyediting: Linda E. Kim

Glass Lyre Press, LLC
P.O. Box 2693
Glenview, IL 60025
www.GlassLyrePress.com

Acknowledgments

Publishers of poems in *The Relentless Pronoun* include:

AGNI, American Literary Review, Art Times, Blue Unicorn, Cincinnati Review, Cumberland Review, Cutbank, Eclipse, 14 Hills, Green Hills Literary Review, Hayden's Ferry, KORE, New Millennium Writings, New Orleans Journal, Nimrod, Meridian, Oxford Magazine, Paris Review, Peregrine, Skid Row Penthouse, Southern Humanities Review, SPEC, Tampa Review, The Literary Review, and *Web Del Sol.*

Many thanks to the Virginia Colony for the Creative Arts for providing time and work-space to write many of the poems in this collection.

Contents

Acknowledgments	iii
Verily Beginning	1
Cat and the Chinese Painting	2
Birding on Key West	3
You Were of Several Minds	4
Gulls	5
Leaving the Apartment Early Because the Heat's Still On	6
Orange Lamp	7
Medusa, Me	8
Forgot, with Trappings	9
Fisher King, Lost Brother	10
Psalm	11
The Relentless Pronoun	12
Failed Faith and the Naked Doll	15
State of Being	16
Surface Phenomena	17
Made in China	18
Putter of Pepper and Salt	19
Half a Cup, Please More	20
If It All Made Sense	21
Form Follows Duty	22
Back Bay Station, Boston	23
Domes Over Istanbul	24
Confessions of a Wednesday Morning	25

Fishing Off Cuttyhunk	29
Ocean Makes Daybreak	30
Berry Basket	31
Ladders Considered	32
You in Your Jelly–Green Shoes	33
Wrack and the Sea	34
Dunes That Day	35
Ogling	36
Dream House	37
Horizons	39
Bice Blue and the Continous Present	43
You Promised	44
Dark Whistle	45
Never Put to Paper	46
What I Missed Telling You	47
Dogged	48
Placing	49
Barely Ask	50
Subjunctive Mood	51
About the Author	53

For Gard

Verily Beginning

Before gates slammed
on our time of naming

bringing syntax and fuss,
before the long journey's parch

scrabbling a place
on hillsides, at the cave's mouth;

before the Great Rain, birds
bitching over scraps,

trees flooded, drownings;
and, before our clotted remorse—

things were liquid
and I heard air in a stone's doze

the world, vague and translucent
when putting my ear to you

I found form.

Cat and the Chinese Painting

Not long after you left you said the cat died
scattering innuendoes like cut ribbons about the room.

Each morning the cat crept out from under your bed,
you said, and went downstairs behind you.

On the step below the painting of a coral Chinese wall,
the cat paused to let you stoop, pet its waiting

submissive neck, which you never failed to do.
The cat would not survive traumatic surgeries,

so you finally had to put her down, then you
went home, you said, and wept. But the hardest

part would be later, on the step beneath the Chinese
painting where you'd reach for the cat to repeat

the pattern, only now stroking empty air. Then you said
It's breaking the habit that's the hardest, and I said, Yes.

Birding on Key West

Stifled by pressed heat of Florida August,
we cut a swath for luring birds and one another.

I took to humming, you to reticence
a royal tern, his florescent white

with black head, slicked wings, orange beak.
You were, by then, long gone.

Who has seen an island's wooden porch
knows the confrontations: home and the sea

man and woman. Make any combination,
two will come together, though not for long

each keeping origins, bated breath
clipped wings, respective feathers.

You Were of Several Minds

I, for one, quite separate. You took to edges, tin motorcycle
caught on the sofa leg and coughing.
                                            We were ungainly,

small things set to undo us as once road dust spun
whirlwinds, hopping the yard
                                            before thunder broke

open everything we had tried to save; echo in the cistern,
cellar flooded. I took to covering.
                                            It was roofing

rain on tin, a comfort, especially in the shed; you, undecided. After
all, random whirl wind, what could be done?
                                            Sticks strewn,

depressions where the litter had gathered; only you
and I knew the summary: how much
                                            repair or winding

up is needed before routine begins again, what's
been scattered, collected – the truth of clutter
                                                  laid bare.

Gulls

Day dreaming between a song sparrow's deft bells
on telephone wires, a mockingbird's commentary

and all our talk, I am thinking we're on a hollow roll,
bewildered, not wholly there. It's a bleached-white day,

only a few dunes up Fisher's Landing to the beach house
taking in noon light over green sea waving,

piping plovers marking the minutes in wily arcs.
This is how to live forever, you say, though there's dissenting

about the bone-gray clapboards, telephone pole's
straggly black hairs looped behind ears where cormorants

droop their tar-pit feathers in a state of resignation.
Take the Hopper painting of a white-washed house

atop some dunes; make it purple with pale blue plaster.
How long will this last? you ask, changing your tune about time.

Meanwhile the gulls come and go: some common,
some Herring, some Black-Backed, some Laughing.

Leaving the Apartment Early Because the Heat's Still On

Gummy heat radiated, slathered on tables, I stand
to withstand solitude, leafings outside on the ash

windows eased open, my mental gambol finally in check;
I said with introspect: The course will not stay thus;

no given equilibrium, however tempered by a shaded
eye, indecorous lamp with circles under, lasting forever;

but soon as I leave the front door behind I am
in the thrall and hest of it all again; walking the block:

pigeons thick as rain, fruit-stand figs with purple cheeks
messes of swaddled papers on the neck of phone poles;

then suddenly I am asking why you came back:
wasn't it enough: our feisty way of holding on to winter

rattled-up pressure from the cellar, penitent steam?
Now what will I do with this, an addled April, you?

Orange Lamp

Remembering the Grecian Urn, China plate, jar on a hill in Tennessee
I regard the plaster cast of an orange lamp in a neighborhood bar

not far from our apartment in an American city; the base is the point:
a grainy replication of two lovers kissing beside a castle tower,

on the other side a leaning woman all alone—piece of brass patina
missing from her lip; the shade shades me in amber ambivalence

watching which way the color will go sliding down the bar, into glasses
and onto faces of drinkers, escapers imagining prosperity

their achievements in the papers, today's solutions --the trenchant
habits of people imbibing and abiding; then the bar tender

pulls the pull chain on the lamp—a metaphysic moment
when the lamp's kissing couple and the woman meet in darkness

unbeknownst and innocent of what's going on along the glassy
surface of the bar and me, eclipsed with a glass almost to my lip.

Medusa, Me

Snake head, they called her and laughed black gums.
Say what you will, ugly is the beholder's fault too.

Pretty is as pretty does, my mother said, when I threw
a fit to have a fur muff, zippered pocket.

How does a mouth say all it wants when hit?
It does like a snake head after it's been severed.

After good deeds and alms-giving, disaster
nothing evens out: a beautiful woman, legless child.

Everything out the window is old-snow
with-dirt. What you want doesn't count

my mother said, but the snakes kept coming
even after everyone thought they were all cut off.

Forgot, with Trappings

for my sister

Things settled to the bottom of a morning, only
worse: you took to bed as Southern ladies do, minus
belongings, baffled as millinery shoppers,

(what to do with grosgrain ribbon, twill piping.)
Shasta daisies in a blue vase, you complained,
nursed along, under round-the-clock surveillance.

Fit to be tied, I said, remembering dimes
knotted in handkerchiefs for the collection plate
dropped as one should: filial obligation.

Awful way to get through: this mincing, this slough
this dalliance and pills (berries on an old hat
or worse) swallowed without a hand.

Remember our Missouri roots, we said,
taciturn, a bit touched, coming down the aisle
as always, with hymnals and wilted lily.

Fisher King, Lost Brother

A dream: worse with monk fish
    swarming brackish water below,
        a surface impossible to swim across
  Is this a river? to someone netting
    large birds (I think: kingfishers)
me, languishing on edges of Truro's
    marsh grass sedge;

Then, almost awake, the Fisher King appears
    samite robe dragging parquet floors,
        gimp leg hung out for someone
to heal the oozing wound,
    all the land parched, rivers black
monk fish swooning maudlin
    circles under a jaundiced moon;

Then remembering: once along a river
    leaves collecting edges like birds
        someone tagged and let go waiting
for next year when my brother
    would not be crying from strange
fevers, someone in the garden
    digging worms, nothing blooming.

To stay in dreams a dangerous pain while the moon
    keeps washing up faces like slung
        monkfish along shores
ropes of seaweed swaddling
    as they carry you back to a king's
disease, bird, lost brother.

Psalm

You, Lord, are my shepherd, imagination
figment; I seek you in patterns of Thanks-
giving tablecloths and in a bristling-
emerald suburban back yard.

I look for you in trout streams and (bless us)
in the eyes of tuna off Baja where Emmy lives.
You hide and promise me restoration.
Even as I survived loss and grieving

I have done so remembering Mother
and her prayers to You, which brings up
Thanksgiving again and the disasters
with my former husband, his anguish

carving the turkey after it separated
from the bone; I go out and weep
in the yard; surely some kind of comfort
will accompany me alone on the way back

to Boston in the car, and surely
you will welcome my soul
someday in a place that I don't know
myself, but that Mother called home.

The Relentless Pronoun

If, in summer's dalliance of screen doors
there's a warp on the last board

so nothing closes right,
you are evasive, aslant,

why do I take up the you burden
carry it all day, suppose

these quibbles will dissolve
in evening's chilled soup?

How is it that across tables, yards, long roads
next towns, cities, the sea

the mass and graining of everything
winds back to you?

Turn over any stone:
after the leaf and downpour

after the feather net of tent moths
the maples in final fade

it's you again, in the whistle,
in the cry.

*

Failed Faith and the Naked Doll

Hold off, off we would in a world where stood a naked doll
and naked frog—about to wait it out, vague, unclear how
natural and superficial could be apart and a part. I had on
a nurse's hat, the rest in temporary uniform for cover.
After the event, the world raced to the pumps, hydrants,
gazebos with no wells. We waited finding unnatural
nothings to do. Take how nurses are supposed
to administer solutions. Well, off the mark. Take a hat too
such a simple interim: waiting on vagaries which we loathe
but must know this: every conductor, every glider.
I'm dragging love by the cap to let it get past regret—
my head in a mattress of clouds that won't lift a whit.

State of Being

Rusted mesh metal roped to the dock—the bait
box held a catfish caught in the neighbor's mucky
rowboat harbor. What happened that day, I have to ask—
when Uncle Ray dumped catch from his creel into the box
as we all watched—that catfish became the catch word
for oddity, attached like an inside pocket to Ray, sly angler,
me, the rapt one with bamboo pole, bait and watery line,
longing for his favor. Years later Ray taught French,
Spanish, and Russian grammar, moved to Uruguay
to find a perfect democracy, drank, recovered, wrote
a book on functions of the verb to be—and shot himself
at the age I am now. So, though you may not
always see it in my eyes, I am in a watery deep—
the hook of him, the worm of what happened.

Surface Phenomena

Now it seems all that falderal,
fumaroles, with the past

in Boston Aquarium's main tank
out of the aqua slides

staring me face to face
as I, embarrassed, sense

from behind glass
evolved and ugly

elbows and lids
given fish-like cerebrum

of course
and the fish

observe how he cruises
for practice as I had

life swimming by
tanked, coy

amounted to nothing;
swimming up like mullet

when
a tilapia

lips moving *oo wah, oo wah,*
my past floating up

no way to coddle, shape it
eyeballs filmed, fins

against all that happens monstrous,
and attachments

which is the difference between us
though he has a few of his own;

the tank's bottom kissing
before so much happened,

like a school of minnows
trying to avoid the mesh sieve.

Made in China

Here's a shoestring day as ambling through forsythia
and shagbark hickory we come to Gloucester's shore;

I don't belong; it's someone else's property; damp hill
slip, slightly swampish. I'm leaf-sogged under sole

fishy too in a pre-historic way, this waterside thicket
where I watch a flock of mergansers and least terns,

air-thin bag caught phlegm-like on a branch,
flattened black inner tube, and one water-logged shoe,

floated from somewhere else, down shore,
or China where factory workers cobble and sew

so many hours, exhausted, they quit at age twenty five,
stumble back to bamboo villages, plastic windows,

history wagging on, needing renewal, though
not incremental, as the future comes crashing

through the bushes, me here, in a shore-view cavity,
trash and all that's heavy on my heart which is metaphor

since who can say how junk comes and goes
rubbery topsider—loosed tongue, lost laces?

Putter of Pepper and Salt

They said keep a stiff upper lip when the cut came,
a thunder of back-slapping rocks and no stopping,

heard as mere tinkling symbols in the aftermath;
then always, when slipping to futures just past,

a ravage of clippings, a sewage of trash
as news finally comes from oceans away:

hip of a mountain gone like a bubble in a tub
where you sit soaking, me in the kitchen

a putter of pepper and salt. What can
happen in a blink of an eye one can't tell

'til rocks and rubble hit your own cottage,
drought dries the well; 'til then mere commotion;

What's well always ends, someone calls to us
down the hallway called time—

toothbrush by the bathroom mirror hung
as reminder how it all wears to bristle and bone.

Half a Cup, Please More

Green glazed diner vinyl counter top hunch
back waiter Heinz red apron squat pepper couple

glass and stained steel pound cake to pulp:
contours of collapse—an abandoned caboose;

diner coffee cup I crossed my heart hoped
for eggs butter sugar in lumps elbows

where bacon smell hovered to serve what purpose
paper hands, forked tongue, bibs of green

laminate trays, incidents of flash and cameo cliché.
I am the diner, reader, I take in I am taken

in by mustard jars and serrated pickle
relish all I tell you, grotesque and dear.

If It All Made Sense

July's spidery sparklers,
checked table cloth, grosgrain grass

red graffiti on water towers
yellowing piano keys

you looking for chicken chunks in soup
rattle of bottles on shelf glass

clothes pins on a line in snow storms
trowel handle lost in the tulips

frowsy robe on a porcelain hook,
toddlers with soap in a sink

bird asleep, cheek down
yellow pencils floating to gutters

warm drips of candle wax
you stirring milk for a custard

pink and black striped socks
the moment the toast pops

stones on the sill,
a screen-door's rusted hasp

worn quilts
bachelor buttons

plastic heart button
belly buttons.

Form Follows Duty

Don't give me that line—perpetual deceits
a string of lies with clothes-pinned conceit

stung from house to house, work pants flapping—
sheets of paper, horizontally flat, over lapping

a margin of truth just inches away from the ledge;
I don't want to think about—the rhythmic edge

where, when reaching to be fluid and fine
the line whines—cams, pulleys, sound twine,

sibilants shushing and hissing around
gutturals like tubas making sound deep

throat-level. Then Oh You which is the line
you use at the votive—the turn away from time

with me, Love, limned, hidden from beauty
by sheets smoothed, pressed to poetic duty.

Back Bay Station, Boston

In the molten whereabouts of my affinities, scrabble of our times, bent
men pushing bottle carts, today and its returns, haphazard, on the way

to the subway I see how the newsstand with its slotted mouth,
chutes to a headline, defining me and the city. Take this morning:

can we tell what's happening, news bites and everyone hungry for more;
can we know what could still happen—wooly weather bits, odoriferous air,

all the drifted children in baskets after so many
rivers gone stale, still waiting to be recovered?

Domes Over Istanbul

Assuming shades of green on a leather hassock set on a carpet of coral, turning at a lackadaisical rate;

me in a lather, mixing caution with cushion in a loggia's mind-spin, my usual yarn of yearning:

bold Turks, gold dome-aspiring sky, above all, a slather of floated boats on a Bosporus azure

was when it all came together, this turning of time, me on the Ottoman my habit of holding on:

spices, trinkets, slice of lime, minarets against the lavender; I put them all in a pocket

(especially the miniscule Mosque) and hoped in the hotel, sequestering could hold off the losses.

Confessions of a Wednesday Morning

My love migrated, picked up its tent, cook pots and bedding,
piled into a cart and moved on.

Imagine Zenobia that great Syrian desert queen
with magnificent buildings captured

packed off to Rome, though she was lucky
a rich senator saved her

whereas mine just keeps wandering dirt roads,
occasional cobbles in small towns.

I follow in my brown skirt, old shoes, sometimes
losing it in poplars along the road

to Odessa whose cobbles above the ancient steps
lead to the Black Sea.

Sometimes I feel it disappear like some genie
that steps out of the story.

It goes off to work in a suit while I'm in the kitchen
carton of Egg Beaters making a low-fat breakfast

with onion, spinach and salt.

*

Fishing Off Cuttyhunk

In the tweezered light between storm and storm

evening's air brushing the sea's purple cheek

silent creatures roiling below: fin fills, bones, lemniscuses

feather gills breathing water when a single hook descends.

Who would not love the desultory darkness

of these hushed emerald-depths?

Who would not take the tessellate gobbet

suspended so seductive on its willy-nilly line

only a fin flick from knowing?

Ocean Makes Daybreak

The ocean makes daybreak
an antique porcelain platter

us wondering whose fault it was—
slivers scattering the sun.

They say waves of high frequencies
can shatter glass if its hand-blown and thin

thinner in after-dinner hours when
the back yard is up to its shins in fire flies,

thinner than the time
we didn't speak for weeks.

How does the sun collect itself after that
and go on with the day's chores,

paying attention to oranges, hammers,
the memory of ant hills in West Africa?

Of course the ocean is always tending us,
refilling our wine glasses like a footman,

gull flying by—stitching the sky closed,
clouds in a pout like they always are.

But we can't say anything, really, about fault
lost as it is in the obscurity of waves

washing back and forth until one breaks
again, albeit resurfacing, part mended.

Berry Basket

Whoever picks berries outside the village
licks fingers for their flavor

and carries the berries home in a basket,
puts them in a bowl, sugars them and floats them

in cream; then, with a silver spoon,
eats them and finds them bitter,

knows the strange empty of the basket
and how the sun rims everything

until it descends slowly into the trees
as shadows shorten, dim, and disappear.

Ladders Considered

Their stretch to high barns
of hay scent, mouse hair, soft landings;

or dark ones to attics
of broke ribboned letters, rusted clocks;

lethargic ones inclined to shop walls
with dangling cans of paint;

spiked tongs on trees for swinging,
under cut-outs of a teal blue sky

rungs on a wooden bridge
across a slathery river:

I love their airy bones
keeping us swept in the rose hoop

of illusion, carrying us to edges
of an imagined, hoped, other side.

You in Your Jelly–Green Shoes

Underwater stones clapped together make muffled clicks:
my hair floating wave-wise in the lake's tourmaline.

Don't lean under the dock with your jellies on, you'll be caught on the barrel-
float wire. And down. Come up for air (an instant) there, there:

stone-water ground down; you alone with the elements, along
with curious finny-tail minnows, silvered blue gills filing by:

submerged history with its halting increments: flatworm, cockle,
urchin, barnacle, snail, salamander—each sundry and assuming.

You could be anyone submerged or short of breath
when the cleft before you is a leap you have to make,

risk of water, cliffs, rocks about to give, lurkers undercover—
the world a sea barge with tarp at a tilt, not quite belly-up.

Wrack and the Sea

In the down dream where I live
gauds are savors and keep:

Andromeda in scaly shoals,
lash and tail dragging seaweed,

Medea, poised on the gunwales
clutching a trunk of odd dresses,

(me too, in my whorl and wait)

all precious little hoards with remnants,
corollaries staving the roar, the undertow.

It does not happen overnight—this holding
on to a love I wish I could keep.

It flies off—a gull with kelp,
in its wallowed mouth,

throwing glitter as he goes.

Dunes That Day

for Sally Landis

Rugarose hedge

        flat faced sand   dunes,

    a moving thought of rusty wind.

I wind and wind string from a kite

        blown through a cloud with a hole

        in my thinking

that could be   moved   as

        even the rabbit with cotton swab

        in orbit through the yard

    out to the edge   of the humming mounds

        soupcons of sand lifted

            came as they did you, Dear

                to be taken away.

We stood by the hedge and could not think;

    it was your yard,   your rose thicket with rabbits

    we loved   your mind   you said

        with holes

            no longer able to hold.

Outside we couldn't see the dunes move

            but they had.

Ogling

Pair of goggles   on a limp shirt   circum-
    stance
        of site   gone under   circa 2010
your stance: agog
    for site of some   thing
        under   way   without me
You, my circum-   chance of
a   life   time   unseen   pair
  past   gone
    goggling
what was   under
   way   what
s'way   back   in time   now
  dogged   summer   screen
or   block   you   hid
what   happened
  after   that   bogged
   and   downed
    out.

Dream House

Before the sea starts   fiddler crabs

               a gargle of skiffs
      swallowing   the scene —

speckled dove
           in cameo   on the harbor-master's house

     shoals   blue sand

turning the mind

        to a house
        of cards
          that   will   and do

    fall

   no fiddlers then.

I'm vagrant   in time to catch   the silhouette

      of the dove
      as the tide turns the world.

First a dream will make a house
then a house will take a turn
become a discarded shell of itself

then fragile   as morning
soars on   becoming
         day.   Decades.

What becomes us   becomes us

You make   a bed   to lie down   in shoals

one day   and become   the sea.

Horizons

Horizon lines fade languorously just past blue
hues you say can't be duplicated—too thin,
too moving the way fog languishes
over Vermont meadows I love hazy, liquid
undefined—as if the planet were losing its heft,
its edges, sliding aside its tectonic plates:
you wanting it kept back-field lilac fresh,
me, sure of our encroaching synthetic fate:
replete with agitated chromosomes
depleted reserves of bituminous, anthracite;
mountain heights reduced, erosions, clones
and a host of carcinogenic corrosives.
Put the dish in the sink, Love, let's let the sun
go down slow tonight—nothing to be done.

*

Bice Blue and the Continous Present

Past perfect
mode of leaving well enough alone,
as in *he had been here but left*
flat hand of what can't be undone—
not by revision, not by adjustment
(door knob screwed tight,
        bracket for the cellar step at last)

Simple past
thinly strung to the present
as in *he was here but left:*
air-borne leaves in updrafts,
dust caught in scratches on old windows:
(key in the Honda lock,
        engine echo in the driveway)

Continuous present
promising the world
as in *he is coming any minute now:*
bice-blue sky with lissome swills
morphing to elephants, rabbits, squirrels:
(everyone romping the lawn,
some with soccer balls)

Continuous future,
as in *he will be coming:* ominous
pause, reluctance in the form
of excuses scribbled on envelops
slipped under the hallway door
(me still looking
        for your return.)

You Promised

Blousy orange October, canary yellow ruffles of sunlight
where air parts, cars slicked down Arlington outside the Ritz,

paten leather limos spilling satin women with clickering heels,
tuxedoed waves to the concierge with suede-gray gloves;

month of oblong and skittery—when one click brings
on another until you're back at a hasp on a porch screen door,

a dropped presser-foot on the Singer that stayed in the basement
'til the house sold, everyone gone, parents deceased;

then you remember the corner drug store's Babe Ruth candy
and sipping cherry Cokes on stool rounds with torn vinyl trim;

Octobers piled like aspen leaves over the Ritz-windowed park
where we first met, kissed and made the promises you broke

though of course there were troubles everywhere—then moving
belongings, bedrooms to basements, ragged toaster, bar stool;

but what are promises anyway: pretends that change like sumac,
fuchsia to brown, park keepers sweeping asters to rusted bins.

I like how air parts and turns a promise to something else
and how, here at the Ritz together, those old days barely matter.

Dark Whistle

Floundering in a country soured by iron-mouth disease,
Pennsylvanian hills lumbered to exhaust, yellow air,
barely a wind to skirt landscapes—limpid, dour;

Floundering on edge when honor fails, heroes
drummed and fifed out, ticker tapes fleeing,
antennae-punctured clouds dripping the water tanks;

Floundering in a strange strafe, bullet holes in bathroom walls
broke sink, whir of copter crickets with eyes to take out,
canister rust, wild screaming armatures;

Floundering in a glut, ersatz park-boulders, steel trees,
finger nails with nuclear dirt, yellow eye of starlings
on the cottonwood turned pulpy, scales on the cypress;

Floundering in a web of eons spun from invisible stuff
colossal in darkness where fields and vectors collapse
or explode as an Arctic iceberg, its dissolving ghost;

Floundering, too, here on an April evening, face cloth
in hand, you in the other room, bevel of a mirror
reflecting an etching of Chartres Cathedral
by the hall clock ticking, kettle steaming,
me in the tilted living room whistling the dark.

Never Put to Paper

You called my swallows, swifts.
Where, in the sea's drum

was the drifting between us,
mysterious green Adriatic below?

I know the swift heart,
dip and risk over petulant waters

how wingspread allows a tentative
sweep before the precipitous drop.

Once, we stayed together:
then invisible intervals,

events between like linens
flying off the hotel laundry line,

falling to cobbles below.
Up here in the hotel room

I want to write a letter
explaining my heart,

its intermittent flight.
But you are right here.

What I Missed Telling You

the way water gives its shadows to high trees,
the way wood yields to signs of patient rot,

the way rain falls on only one side of the road,
the way mud slumps the edge of river beds,

the way a jay reluctantly leaves the best limb,
the way osprey cry when fleeing home;

the way one leaf whirls and others stay still,
the way a stone loosens and falls only so far,

the way lilies bend long necks to find the sun,
the way the sun makes glitter of snail trails,

the way the moon turns transparent in daylight,
the daylight turns phosphorescent in autumn,

the way children slosh boots in rain puddles,
the way old men swing their arms when walking on sand,

the way kite strings sag in the middle,
stars hang in the night sky without a hook,

the way fish hooks are so hard to remove.

Dogged

Two dogs tied to a Boston lamppost
sniff and grieve, one with shabby ears,
sad eyes, the other superficially frisky,
the sad one gazing longingly
at Starbuck's window where his master
blithely buys a lemon muffin.

Well, you can't do both, you say, but I say
sadness is everywhere—in December's
thawed puddles, in the drip drip at the end
of the down spout where the corrugated
neck leans on the yard's chipped curb,
my heart tied to the lamp post of you.

Placing

We swim in slurries of unhinged words
trying to explain how this could happen
                                (rebus in reverse)
relying on cultivated memories
                                that never agree
                                like unmatched flowers
                                on a faded dress.

I think what really happened that day: he
was fixing something on the boat at the dock,
                                wadded sisal knots
slowing the work down—him not noticing
she was gone the way
dandelion spore,
                              float-off so quiet.

So why do we tell this over and over
on the porch, by the bench, in the garden,
our stories never
agreeing - never needled and stitched properly,
                              never mending
                              nothing whole again.

We need a place to get our bearings—
there always being reasons to malinger
pause before finding a right place
to put the pincushion
that needs attention, placed so
carefully in its
homely drawer.

Barely Ask

When you get old do your lips shrink, do you know?
I don't know do your lips thin when you get old,

do they draw to a pink line, do they together get smaller
I don't know do you? Do your lips together know

when you get old, do you know together when
you get old if your lips when pressed get an answer?

Do your lips pressed together know together a small
answer or no answer at all when you get old? Do you

press for an answer at all when you get old? Do you
press for a small answer or maybe no answer, as one

pressed to another might know lips' way to know
or do you together know what is too small to answer

when you are too old to talk or talk is too small
for questions you know you could answer but

your lips tell you not to answer just stay together.

Subjunctive Mood

How do we discuss our riven
and lost certainties, habits:
my search for you – your
off-edges, our took chances,
as if we would
given conditions and our earthly ties,
time angled past old perimeters,
us, addled in museums and poems,
rubber canvas, stretched verse
      as if we could
seeing how language works
volant like field creatures
in their burrow and stash
trying to hold what was
      or could have been.

About the Author

Lynne Potts has two previous collections of poetry published by National Poetry Review Press, one for which she won the book prize in 2012.

Individual poems have appeared in *Denver Quarterly, The Paris Review, New American Writing, American Literary Review, Georgia Review, New Millenium Writings* and elsewhere. Awards include Massachusetts Cultural Council, Ragdale, and Virginia Colony for the Arts (VCCA) fellowships. She is Poetry Editor at AGNI, and lives in both Boston and New York.

Glass Lyre Press

exceptional works to replenish the spirit

Glass Lyre Press is an independent literary publisher interested in technically accomplished, stylistically distinct, and original work. Glass Lyre seeks diverse writers that possess a dynamic aesthetic and an ability to emotionally and intellectually engage a wide audience of readers.

Glass Lyre's vision is to connect the world through language and art. We hope to expand the scope of poetry and short fiction for the general reader through exceptionally well-written books, which evoke emotion, provide insight, and resonate with the human spirit.

Poetry Collections
Poetry Chapbooks
Select Short & Flash Fiction
Anthologies

www.GlassLyrePress.com

www.ingramcontent.com/pod-product-compliance
Lightning Source LLC
Chambersburg PA
CBHW021452080526
44588CB00009B/813